This Is
What
LOVE
Is

**The Most Romantic Quotes
& Poems Which Capture
The Rapture Of Love**

by Dan & Dave Davidson

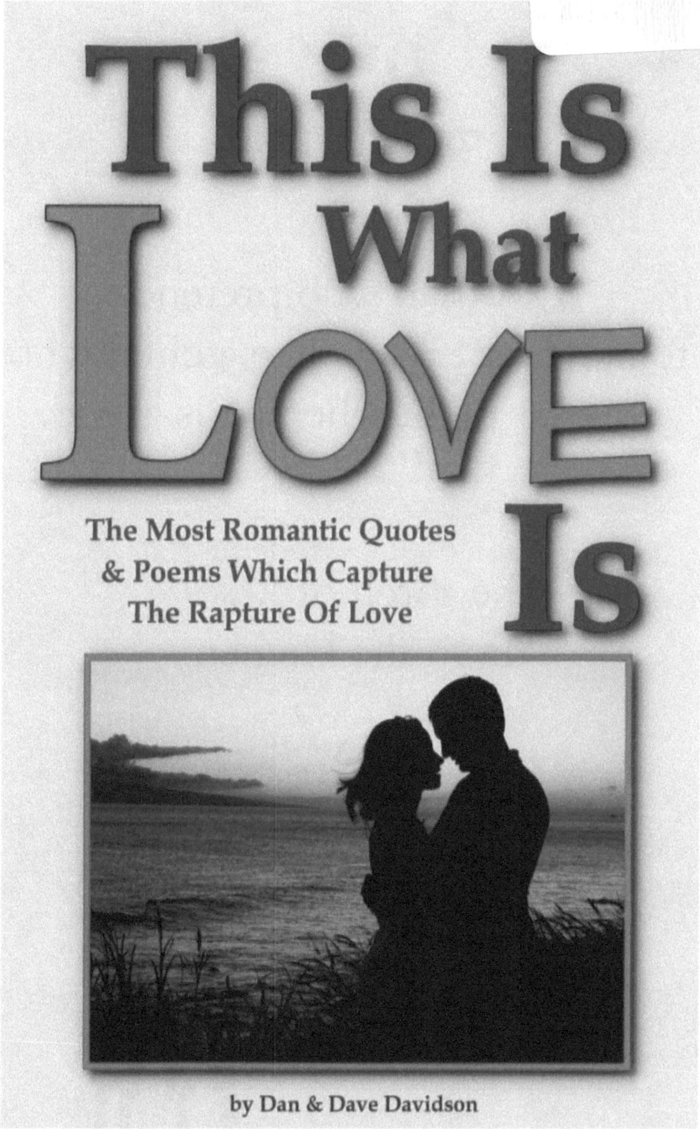

© 2001 & 2013 by brothers Dan & Dave Davidson
all photography © Dave Davidson
DaveDavidson.com

Love is
the only gold.

Tennyson

A woman who pretends
to laugh at love is like a child who
sings at night when he is afraid.

Unknown

The torch of love is
lit in the kitchen.

French Proverb

Love is

in the poetry, the music, the flowers,
the perfume, the dancing, the moonlight sky,
the slow burning fire, the shimmering dresses,
the smoothest of men, the eye batting beauty,
the ocean by morning, the tender kisses at night,
the long flowing tendrils, the way he says my name,
the mountains in winter, the sunset's water
reflection. All these possibilities feed your
romantic spirit and keep it alive.

Becca Lynn

Love is
friendship set on fire.

Jeremy Taylor

Love is

a butterfly which,
when pursued is just
beyond your grasp, but if
you will sit down quietly,
it may alight upon you.

Nathaniel Hawthorne

Love is

bright photosynthesis,
bringing affection to light
with a well watered kiss.

Dave Davidson

True love is like ghosts,
which everybody talks about
and few have seen. If one judges
love by the majority of its effects,
it is more like hatred than friendship.
There is no disguise which can hide
love for long where it exists or
simulate it where it does not.

Francis De La Rochefoucauld

Where love is concerned,
too much is not even enough.

Pierre-Augustin De Beaumarchais

Love is

an image of God. . .
the living essence of
the divine nature which
beams full of all goodness.

Martin Luther

Love is

a mutual admiration society consisting
but of two members. . . the one whose
love is less intense will become president.

Joseph Mayer

Love is blind.

Geoffrey Chaucer

Love is all we have, the only way that each can help the other.

Euripedes

Love is
is not rude,
it is not self seeking,
it is not easily angered,
it keeps no record of wrongs.
Love does not delight in evil
but rejoices in truth.
It always protects,
always trusts,
always hopes,
always perseveres.

1 Corinthians 13:5&6

Love is
as much of
an object as
an obsession,
everybody wants it,
everybody seeks it,
but few ever achieve it,
those who do will cherish it,
be lost in it, and among all,
never...never forget it.

Curtis Judalet

Love is

much like a wild rose,
beautiful and calm,
but willing to draw
blood in its defense.

Mark Overby

Love is

a perky elf dancing
a merry little jig
and then suddenly
he turns on you
with a miniature
machine gun.

Matt Groening

Love is

swinging and swaying,
cuddling cozy together
on a net mesh hammock
allowing room to breath
in the summer breeze.

Dave Davidson

Love is

not knowing
how you feel
and not feeling
what you know.

John Dough

Love is

a great beautifier

Louisa May Alcott

Love is

a pleasant surprise
scheduled in disguise.

Cyrano De Words-u-lac

Love is

a canvas furnished by
nature and embroidered
by imagination.

Voltaire

The secret of love is seeking variety in your life together, and never letting routine chords dull the melody of your romance.

Unknown

Love is

is a pin cushion
taking its stabs,
yet still appearing
fuzzy wuzzy.

Hugh Myrrh

Love is

the passion of hearts,
the language of poetry
and the entertainment
of drama mixed with
the mystery of fiction.

Dave Davidson

Love is

a candlelight dinner
aboard a speed boat.

Hugh Myrrh

Love is

being a bridge's beam
in someone else's dream.

Cyrano De Words-u-lac

Love is

like quicksilver in the hand.
Leave the fingers open and it stays.
Clutch it, and it darts away.

Dorothy Parker

Love is

a candlelight dinner
aboard a speed boat.

Hugh Myrrh

Love is not love
until love's vulnerable.

Theodore Roethke

Love is

a haunting thing to keep on remembering if it never occurs.

Dave Davidson

Love is a kind of warfare.

OVID

Love is

not an emptiness
longing to be filled-
it is a fullness pressing
to be released.

J. Kennedy Shultz

Love is

a long lasting battery
that needs regular recharging.
Ironically dim lighting is a
great recharging method.

Dave Davidson

Love is

heartburn
without the chili.

Hugh Myrrh

Love is
watching the sunset
with your spouse then
closing the blinds to miss
the sunrise together.

Diane Gammon

Love is a recipe that spoils everyone at the
table sometimes to the point of a bellyache.

Dave Davidson

Love is

a ghastly wine freshening
and fortifying the minds of
its chosen, and raising them
beyond thought or care
of worldy allurements.

Richard Rolle

Love is
the more subtle
form of self-interest.

Holbrook Jackson

Love is
the wisdom of the fool
and the folly of the wise.

Samuel Johnson

Love is
always revolutionary.

Andrei Voznesensky

Love is
sentimental
measles.

Charles Kingsley

Love is

not just stopping
to smell sweet roses...
its pausing to pick, prune
and put them in a vase.

Dave Davidson

To love is to choose.

Joseph Roux

Love is

an art of the heart,
not a science; though
experimenting is
recommended.

Dave Davidson

Love is patient,
love is kind.
It does not envy,
it does not boast,
it is not proud.

1 Corinthians 13:4

Love is

is a pop quiz
graded on
a curve.

Hugh Myrrh

Love is

a passionate perfume
blooming everyday
like a fresh bouquet.

Dave Davidson

Love is

never missing a try
at kissing goodbye.

Cyrano De Words-u-lac

To be in love
is the dearest wish,
the most welcoming dream
and brightest aspiration
a heart can hope for.

Becca Lynn

Love is

a capricious creature
which desires everything
and can be contented
with almost nothing.

Madeline De Scudery

Love is

simply a kiss
smiling together
up close.

Dave Davidson

Love is

a delightful day's journey.
At the farther end kiss your
companion and say farewell.

Ambrose Bierce

To be in love is merely to be in a
state of perceptual anesthesia.

H.L. Mencken

Love is never ever quitting
a promise made on love.

Dave Davidson

Love is
a shot at the buzzer,
as the crowd's curiosity
suspends in time's anticipation.
But all along you knew it was true
when the ball left your hands.

Hugh Myrrh

Of all forms of caution,
caution in love is perhaps
the most fatal to true happiness.

Bertland Russel

Love is

a vivacious verb
nudging a nervous noun,
captured by amorous
agile adjectives.

Dave Davidson

Love is

most nearly itself
when here and now
cease to matter.

T.S. Eliot

Love is
what you've been
through with somebody.

James Thurber

Love is
a reality in the domain
of the imagination.

Charles de Tallleyrand

Love is a music video.

Hugh Myrrh

Love is

the strange bewilderment
which overtakes one person on
account of another person.

James Thurber & E.B. White,

Real love is a pilgrimage.
It happens when there is no strategy,
but it is very rare because most
people are strategists.

Anita Brookner

Love is

the triumph of
imagination over
intelligence.

H.L. Mencken

Love is

what melts Winter
with the warmth
of a Spring kiss.

Dave Davidson

Love is dreamy
and daring,
dangerous and
delicate,
intricate and
intimate.

Dave Davidson

Love is

a kiss rekindling;
Just as sticks rub together-
sparks fly, flames arise,
warmth is nurtured,
passion created.

Dave Davidson

Love is

never genuine if forced,
so one must commit the other's
response to the power of time,
prayer and patience.

Becca Lynn

Love is

a game you win
by letting another
always be first.

Dave Davidson

Love is kindest,
and hath most strength,
The kisses are most sweet,
When it's enjoyed in heat of strength,
Where like affections meet.

Patrick Hannay

Love is
a picnic with ants
crawling up your pants
making you want to dance.

Dave Davidson

Love is blinding.
That is why lovers
like to touch.

German Proverb

Love is

a blessing requiring
capture when bequeathed
and should never be taken
for granted when gravity
falls deep beneath.

Dave Davidson

Love is

a seasoned spice
becoming sweeter
when mixed with
forgiveness.

Dave Davidson

Love is
the beginning,
the middle,
and the end of
everything.

Jean B. Lacordaire

Love is
when she lets you take
a photo of her and you end
up using the whole film.

Michael Boniwell

Love is
lightning and thunder
on a sunny summer afternoon
and bright rays of welcomed
warm light during a storm;
Love...can change
the weather.

Dave Davidson

Love is

not love which
alters when it
alteration finds.

Shakespeare

Love is

often right
under your nose
like a Spring sneeze
blowing in the breeze
from a wild rose.

Dave Davidson

Love is…desiring to
give what is our own to
another and feeling his
delight as our own.

Robert A. Heinlein & Emanuel Swedenborg

Love is

a lot like lunch.
Both are needed everyday,
each start with the letter L,
and you can have
either in bed.

Smart Alex

Love is

simultaneously
proper nutrition and
a delectable dessert.

Dave Davidson

Love is

giving away umbrellas
then getting caught
in refreshing rain
while showers
drench all
over you.

Dave Davidson

If at first, love is dealt
its then a kiss is truly felt.

Cyrano De Words-u-lac

All love is sweet, given or returned.
They who inspire it are fortunate, but
those who feel it most are happier still.

Percy Shelly

Kisses kept are wasted;
Love is to be tasted.

E. V. Cooke

Love is
a symphony appetizer
in a gorgeous flower garden
laughing at a cologne concert,
wearing kaleidoscope shoes.
Love is a journey of
sensational senses.

Dave Davidson

Love is
always assumed crazy
unless its you and me.

Cyrano De Words-u-lac

Love is
the most terrible,
and also the most generous
of all the passions; it is the only
one which includes in the dreams
the happiness of someone else.

Alphone Karr

Love is

a conflict between
reflexes and reflections.

Magnus Hirschfeld

Love is

a risky gambler's heart
who affords challenge.

Dave Davidson

Love is

two minds without
a single thought.

Philip Barry

Love is
either a slap in the face
or a kiss on the cheek.

Dave Davidson

Romance is the icing,
but love is the cake.

Unknown

No one in love is free,
or wants to be.

Unknown

Love is like the moon,
when it does not increase,
it decreases.

Segur

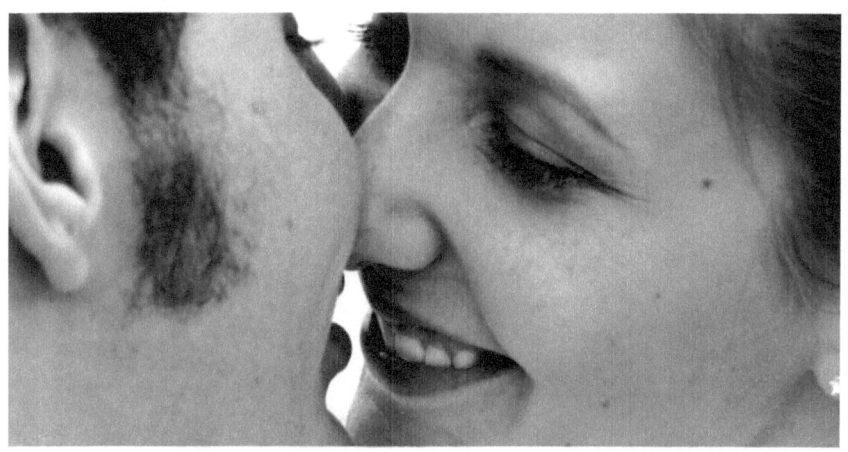

Love is the child of illusion
and the parent of disillusion.

Miguel de Unamuno

Love is trying to dance
without stepping on your
partner's toes.

Dave Davidson

Love is

sharing an intimate secret
in front of a fireplace crackling,
with two mugs of hot chocolate
in a romantic winter scene.

Dave Davidson

41

Love is
a warm hand
on a cool night.

Don Witmer

Love is
a tuxedo rental
repeated, revived,
renewed, recycled
and ready to thrive.

Dave Davidson

Love is
never having to
say you're sorry.

Eric Segal

Love is
the daily delight
and bright sunlight
of tenderness and
forgiveness.

Dave Davidson

Love is

a second life;
It grows into the soul,
warms every vein and
beats in every pulse.

Joseph Addison

Love is

supreme and
unconditional.

Duke Ellington

Love is

allowing separateness
in your togetherness.

Diane Gammon

Love is

the enchanted dawn
of every heart.

Alphonse de Lamartine

I used to check off
my list to see what I missed,
…looking for hearts off a grocery list.
I'm not too sure what love is anymore.

Matt Malyon

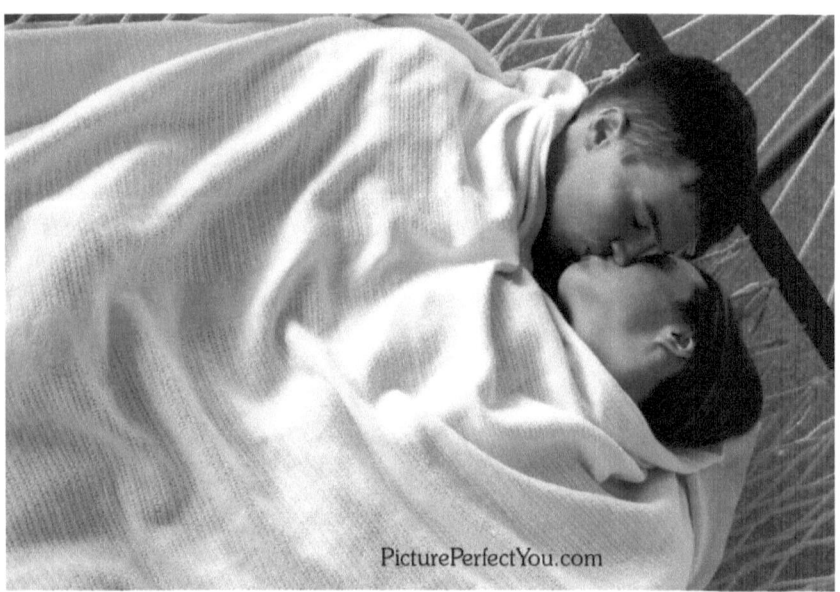

PicturePerfectYou.com

Love is

but the discovery
of ourselves in others,
and the delight in
the recognition.

Alexander Smith

Love is

born with the pleasure
of looking at each other,
it is fed with the necessity
of seeing each other, it is
concluded with the
impossibility of
separation.

Jose Marti Y Perez

Love is

the greatest
refreshment in life.

Pablo Picasso

Love is

what you've
been through
with someone.

James Thruber

Love is

a hand made gift.

Diane Gammon

Love is

a lot like jelly beans.
You have eat bad ones
to enjoy the good ones.

Teresa Zuidema

Love is

the only game that is not
called because of darkness.

Anonymous

Love is

above all, the gift of oneself.

Jean Anouilh

Love is
like chocolate
you can taste
with your heart
when kissing.

Dave Davidson

Love is
a mystery which,
when solved,
evaporates.

Ned Noren

The hidden risk in love is
like walking a tightrope while
over Niagara Falls or wading
knee high kissing in a country
stream. It's the fear of heights
mixed with a cool quenching
of love's delicate desire.

Dave Davidson

Love is

something like the clouds
that were in the sky before
the sun came out.

You cannot touch the clouds,
you know; but you feel the rain
and know how glad the flowers
and the thirsty earth are to have
it after a hot day.

You cannot touch love either;
but you feel the sweetness that
it pours into everything.

Annie Sullivan

Love is
a perpetual hyperbole

Francis Bacon

Love is
the union of a want
and a sentiment.

Honore de Balzac

Perfect love is rare indeed...
To be a lover will require that you
continually have the subtlety of the
very wise, the flexibility of the child,
the sensitivity of the artist, the
understanding of the philosopher,
the acceptance of the saint, the
tolerance of the scholar, and
the fortitude of the certain.

Leo Buscaglia

Falling in love is something
you forget like pain.

Nina Bawden

Love is
a fan club with
only two fans.

Adrian Henri

Love is

a screenplay performed
out on Broadway stage where
each actor and actress are also
writers, directors, producers
and stage hands.

Dave Davidson

Love is

surfing without a board
and bungee jumping
without a chord.

Hugh Myrrh

Love is

transparent,
yet full of color;
A reflecting rainbow
that cannot be held.

Dave Davidson

Love is

a dictionary and
thesaurus with the
pages all glued
together.

Hugh Myrrh

Love is …to commit
oneself without guarantee,
to give oneself completely
in the hope that our love
will produce love in
the loved person.

Erich Fromm

Love is

a gracious
and beautiful art.

Havelock Ellis

Love is

to stop comparing.

Bernard Grasset

Love is

at first sight only realizing
an imagination that has
always haunted us.

William Hazlitt

Love is

to communicate to the other
that you are all for him, that you
will never fail him or let him down
when he needs you, but that you
will always be standing by with all
the necessary encouragements.

Ashley Montague

Love is

the business of the idle,
but the idleness of the busy.

Edward G. Bulwer-Lytton

Love is
sensational,
but not senseless.

Love is vulnerable,
but not irresponsible.

Love is innocent,
but never lacks respect.

Love is romantic,
thriving best in reality.

Love is defenseless,
protecting the best within us.

Love is a way of happiness,
but not its exclusive avenue.

Dave Davidson

Love is

the affirmative of affirmatives.

Ralph Waldo Emerson

Love is

not altogether a delirium,
yet it has many points
in common.

Thomas Carlyle

Love is

a comedian who jokes fun,
but never pokes fun at anyone.

Hugh Myrrh

Love is

making a choice to continue
making the choice to love true.

Cyrano De Words-u-lac

Love is

a telephone wire intertwining
those distance deprives.

Dave Davidson

Love is for fools wise enough
to take a chance.

Amy Grant, Wayne Kirpatrick & Michael W. Smith

Love is

answering all love asks,
taking off small masks.

Cyrano De Words-u-lac

Love is

dreamy and daring,
dangerous and delicate,
comfortable and cautious,
intricate and intimate.

Dave Davidson

Love is

sure and at its best
when pure and honest.

Cyranos De Words-u-lac

Love is

that two solitudes protect
and touch and greet each other.

Rainer M. Rilke

Love is

to believe, to hope, to know
--a taste of heaven below.

Adapted from Edmund Waller

Love is

space and time
measured by the heart.

Marcel Proust

Love is

the fairest and most
profitable guest a reasonable
creature can entertain.

Richard Role

Love is

a little haven of refuge
from the world.

Bernard A. Russell

Love is

a wedding day in May,
a honeymoon in June
and never doubting
why ever in July.

Dave Davidson

Love is

when a person's. . .
own boundary expands
to include the you, the other,
that was previously outside himself.

Fredereick S. Peris

Love is

the mood of believing in miracles.

John C. Powys

Love is

the association of two beings
for the benefit of one.

Countess Nathalie

Love is a mutual misunderstanding.

Oscar Wilde

Love is
the reduction
of the universe
to a single being,
the expansion of
a single being.

Victor Hugo

Love is

an expression of
the communion
between persons.

Thomas Merton

Love is

renunciation of
one's personal comfort.

Leon Tolstoy

Love is

the true means by which
the world is enjoyed.

Thomas Traherne

Love is

an act of endless forgiveness,
a tender look which
becomes a habit.

Peter Ustinov

Love is
never missing
a chance to add
a bit of sunshine
in someone's life.

Diane Gammon

Love is
not getting, but giving.

Henry Van Dyke

Love is
the heart's immortal thirst
to be completely known
and all forgiven.

Henry Van Dyke

Love is
singing a solo of the
Star Spangled Banner
in front of one person
day after day after day.

Dave Davidson

Love is

that condition in
which the happiness
of another person
is essential to
your own joy.

George Eliot

Love is

of all the passions
the strongest, for it attacks
simultaneously the head,
the heart and the senses.

Voltaire

Love is

an irresistible desire
to be irresistibly
desired.

Robert Frost

For love is as strong as death,
its jealousy unyielding as the grave.
It burns like blazing fire like a mighty flame.

Many waters cannot quench love;
rivers cannot wash it away.

Songs Of Songs 8:6,7

Love is

. . . sentiment. . .
the universal thirst
for a communion
not merely of the senses,
but of our whole nature.

Percy Bysshe Shelley

Love is

a gross exaggeration of
the difference between
one person and
everybody else.

George Bernard Shaw

Love is

the supreme value around
which all moral values can be
integrated into one ethical system
valid for the whole of humanity.

Pitrim Sorokin

Love is

in its very essence is liberty:
it is compatible neither with
obedience, jealousy, nor fear:
it is. . . most pure, perfect, and
unlimited where its votaries
live in confidence, equality,
and unreserve.

Percy Bysshe Shelley

Love is

made by two
people, in different
kinds of solitude.

Jose-Pierre Louis Aragon

Love is

to a match,
as lips are to
striking it's
scratch.

Cyrano De Words-u-lac

Love in your heart
wasn't put there to stay.
Love isn't love till you
give it away.

Oscar Hammerstein 2

Love is

a little foolishness
and a lot of curiosity.

George Bernard Shaw

Love is

a spirit all compact of fire.

William Shakespeare

Love is

looking outward together
in the same direction.

Antoine de Saint-Expire

We always
believe our first
love is our last, and
our last love our first.

George Whyte-Melville

The giving of love is
an education in itself.

Eleanor Roosevelt

Love is always in the
mood of believing in miracles.

John Cowper Powys

The most powerful symptom
of love is a tenderness which
becomes at times almost
insupportable.

Victor Hugo

Love is
eternal and enduring,
constant and continuous,
endearing and everlasting.

Rose Angelo

Love is when you remember
her birthday. Even though you had
to write a note to yourself and stick
it on the dashboard of your car.

Michael Boniwell

Love is the master key that opens the
gates of happiness.

Oliver Wendell Holmes

Love is friendship
that has caught fire!

Ann Landers

Youth's for an hour,
beauty's a flower, but love is
the jewel that wins the world.

Moira O'Neill

To love is to admire
with the heart; to admire
is to love with the mind.

Gautier

If I know what love is,
it is because of you.

Herman Hesse

Love is

when, for no reason,
you see mundane things that
have always been there and
find them beautiful.

Michael Boniwell

Love is

the blinding revelation
that some other being
can be more important to
love than he is to himself.

J.V. Casserley

Love is

either the shrinking remnant
of something which was once
enormous; or…part of something
which will grow in the future into
something enormous.

Anton Chekhov

Love is

a symbol of eternity.
It wipes out all sense of time,
destroying all memory of a
beginning and all fear of and end.

Anna Louise de Stael

Love is always enough
when the going gets tough.

Cyrano De Words-u-lac

Love is blonde.

John Donut

Love is

an attempt to change
a piece of the dream
world into reality.

Theodore Roethke

Love is like the
magic touch of stars.

Walter Benton

Love is a little word.
Those in love make it big!

Author Unknown

Love is the only
weapon we need.

Rev. H. R. L. Sheppard

The fate of love is that it always seems too little or too much.

Amelia Barr

Love is

telling someone
you love them.

Dave Davidson

Love is

the gross exaggeration
of the difference between one
person and everyone else.

George Bernard Shaw

Love is

as personal and private
as the one you love.

Hugh Myrrh

Can love really be satisfied
with such polite affections?
To love is to burn...
Can he really love her?
Can the soul really be satisfied
with such polite affections?
To love is to burn, to be
on fire, all full of passion...

Marianne in Sense and Sensibility (1995)
adapted screen play by Emma Thompson

Love is
man's attempt to no longer think.

G. Bennett

Love is
dreaming about the one
you love, only awake and find
they are next to you.

Dave Davidson

Love is
the adaptation and cooperation of
toothpaste tube squeezing methods.

Hugh Myrrh

Love is

the desire of forthcomings
the acceptance of shortcomings,
and approval of homecomings.

Dave Davidson

Applause may be
good for the moment,
but love is everlasting.

Pepe in Adventures of Pinocchio, (1996)

Love is
where reality seeks reverie,
fantasy finds fact a facade,
and dreams are lifelike.

Dave Davidson

Love is
either a drag strip,
or a marathon; for love
is always a race.

Dave Davidson

Love is
the affinity of intimacy,
the rhapsody of ecstasy,
and the tenderness
of sensuousness.

Dave Davidson

Love is

like a police car with
sirens and flashing lights.
And after the initial inspection
sometimes you're taken in.

Dave Davidson

To love and win is the best thing.
To love and lose, the next best.

William M. Thackeray

To fear love is to fear life,
and those who fear life are
already three parts dead.

Bertrand Russell

Love is the
result, reflex,
reward, reprise;
the recipe, reverie,
reception, reverence
refining, reflection;
the refreshment,
and responsibly,
the reinvestment,
and resemblance;
the rejuvenation,
and revelation,
of love.

Dave Davidson

Love is
a distracted
back massage.

Dave Davidson

Love is
never demanding
and always understanding.

Cyrano De Words-u-lac

Love is

feeling home sweet home
when a winter storm
is forecasted.

Dave Davidson

Love anything and your heart
will be wrung and possibly broken.
If you want to make sure of keeping
it intact you must give it to no one,
not even an animal. Wrap it carefully
round with hobbies and little luxuries;
avoid all entanglements. Lock it up
safe in the casket or coffin of your
selfishness. But in that casket - safe,
dark, motionless, airless - it will change.
It will not be broken; it will become
unbreakable, impenetrable, irredeemable.
To love is to be vulnerable.

C.S. Lewis

Love is a promise,
love is a souvenir,
once given never forgotten,
never let it disappear.

John Lennon

Love is a rare opportunity
and when that love is somehow
parted it's something deep down
inside that wants just a reminder,
a slice of memory, a possession.

Unknown

Love is hoping true romance
finds true commitment.

Dave Davidson

Love is
a fast track day at work,
met with slow kiss hello.

Dave Davidson

A woman who pretends
to laugh at love is like a child who
sings at night when he is afraid.

anonymous

All you need is love.

John Lennon

Love is
full of emotion,
you experience
a wonderful feeling,
Like a trip through the ocean
or a voyage through our living.
One day a wave told me:
"If your love is true,
not even the strongest sea
would separate you two."

Pat from Barranquilla

Love is

calling off work
because you're in love.

Dave Davidson

Love is

something eternal;
the aspect may change,
but not the essence.

Aristotle

Life is the flower
for which love is
the honey.

Oliver Wendell Holmes

Love is

a fruit in season at all times,
and within reach of every hand.

Mother Teresa

The truth is that there is
only one terminal dignity - love.
And the story of a love is not important -
what is important is that one is capable of
love. It is perhaps the only glimpse
we are permitted of eternity.

Vincent Van Gogh

Falling in love is drowning
in your deepest thoughts.
Nothing else matters, except
your wonderful love.

Petrach

Love is
a New Year's Eve kiss at
the stroke of midnight.

Dave Davidson

Love is
a mirror that reveals secrets,
refines perception, and reflects
reality into romance.

Dave Davidson

Love is
a steamy window
on a foggy night.

Dave Davidson

Where we love is home,
home that our feet may leave,
but not our hearts.

Victor Hugo

First love is only a little
foolishness and a lot of curiosity.

George Bernard Shaw

Love is

discovering a new side of yourself while sharing the shadow of another.

Dave Davidson

Love is composed of a single soul inhabiting two bodies.

Helen Hayes

Love is

a solemn embrace
which melts into giggles
over an inside joke.

Dave Davidson

Love is

a combination of
sex and sentiment.

Emile Herzog

Love is
when the car breaks down
in the middle of nowhere
and rather than complaining
she starts kissing you instead.

Michael Boniwell

Love is a respectful plumber
who wears a belt to work.

Hugh Myrrh

Love is when she grips your arm
during the scary bits of the movie.

Michael Boniwell

Love is when you walk through the park at
night and she says "I feel so safe with you".

Michael Boniwell

To be able to say how much you love is to
love but little.

Schikaneder, Emanuel

Love is

self destructing
if you're paranoid.

G. Bennett

Love is

saying goodbye
and returning moments later.

Dave Davidson

Love is

a husband and wife taking up
only one fourth of a king sized bed.

Dave Davidson

Love is not blind,
We all could confess;
It sees fault and flaw,
yet never does mind.
Love looks to bless.
Love is not blind,
It sees more not less;
Love can break the law
yet clues never find
answers to its success.

Dave Davidson

Love is like a Rubik's Cube, there are
countless numbers of wrong twists and turns,
but when you get it right, it looks perfect
no matter what way you look at it.

Franklin P. Jones

Love doesn't make the world go round.
Love is what makes the ride worthwhile.

H. Jackson Brown, Jr.

If love is music in its purest form,
then you are the notes on the page
and the melody in my heart.

Les Harris

Love is like swallowing hot chocolate
before it has cooled off. It takes
you by surprise at first, but keeps
you warm for a long time.

Krystal Esplin

Love is indeed blind, offering it's affliction
to lovers willing to lose glasses, toss canes,
walk into walls and lie in the dark.

Hugh Myrrh

Love is the difficult realization that something other than oneself is real.

Iris Murdoch

Love is a fruit in season at all times, and within the reach of every hand.

Pablo Picasso

If love is a drop, I'll send you shower;
If love is a petal, I'll send you flower;
If love is water, I'll send you the sea;
If love is a person, I'll send you me.

Heer

Love is forgetting yourself, letting go into the arms of someone who is there remembering to catch you. That's why it's called falling in love.

Dave Davidson

Love is a fierce competition.
Marriage ends that competition,
commencing a commitment
of no longer competing.

Dave Davidson

Love is the most beautiful of dreams
and the worst of nightmares.

Shakespeare

Love is the great miracle cure.
Loving ourselves works
miracles in our lives.

Mother Theresa

A good **love is** delicious,
you can't get enough too soon.

Jewel Kilcher

Love... What is love?
Love is to love someone for
who they are, who they were,
and who they will be.

Chris Moore

Love is a wild bird that no one can tame.
It's useless to chase it if it won't play the game.

Carmen

Love is the magician that pulls
man out of his own hat.

Ben Hecht

Love is waking up at day break
feeling the embrace of last night's
caresses blanket your body.

Isabel Maria

Love is always open arms.
If you close your arms about love you will find that you are left holding only yourself.

Lord Byron

Love is the ultimate outlaw.
It just won't adhere to any rules.
The most any of us can do is sign on as its accomplice.

Voltaire

Love is enjoying a walk in the rain together. Rarely does walking in the rain alone produce any mushy gushy feelings.

Dave Davidson

Love is a cunning weaver of fantasies and fables.

Sappho

Love is a conflict between reflexes and reflections.

Magnus Hirchfield

An old man in **love is** like a flower in winter.

Portuguese Proverb

When **love is** not madness, it is not love.

Pedro Calderon de la Barca

Love is merely madness...

William Shakespeare

Love is a battlefield.

Pat Benetar

Love is like a shadow,
when you chase it, it runs away,
when you turn back and walk away,
it follows you.

Don Nguyen

Love is the power to touch a heart
regardless of getting to touch a person.
Love is often about feeling a heart's touch.

Dave Davidson

A life without love is like a year without summer.

Swedish Proverb

Love is the seed of all hope.
It is the enticement to trust,
to risk, to try, to go on.

Gloria Gaither

Never pretend to a love which you do not
actually feel, for love is not ours to command.

Alan Watts

True Love is eternal, infinite, and always
like itself. It is equal and pure, without violent
demonstrations: it is seen with white hairs
and is always young in the heart.

John Keats

Such is the inconsistency of real love, that it is
always awake to suspicion, however unreasonable;
always requiring new assurances from
the object of its interest.

Ann Radcliffe

To fear love is to fear life, and those who
fear life are already three parts dead.

Bertrand Russell

Love is the poetry of the senses.

Honoré de Balzac

Love is a story that haunts
you if hearts were mistreated.

Dave Davidson

Love is a game that two can play and both win.

Eva Gabor

Love is a drive through car wash
with loose noodle arms of affection,
spraying showers of passion and hot air
blowing and the end of the ride.

Hugh Myrrh

Love is like those second-rate hotels
where all the luxury is in the lobby.

Paul-Jean Toulet

To love and win is the best thing.
To love and lose, the next best.

William Makepeace Thackeray

All **love is** probationary, a fact which frightens women and exhilarates men.

Mignon McLaughlin

Some say that true **love is** a mirage; seek it anyway, for all else is surely desert.

Robert Brault

Love is the greatest touch-up artist of all.

Robert Brault

Love is an exploding cigar we willingly smoke.

Lynda Barry

Love is an ocean of emotions entirely surrounded by expenses.

Lord Dewar

Love is the word used to label the sexual excitement of the young, the habituation of the middle-aged, and the mutual dependence of the old.

John Ciardi

Love is an electric blanket with somebody else in control of the switch.

Cathy Carlyle

Love is the one thing that still stands when all else has fallen.

Malot

Love is a key that opens doors to both gratification and grief and a window leading to both ecstasy and abandon.

Dave Davidson

Love is never lost. If not reciprocated it will flow back, and soften and purify the heart.

Washington Irving

Love is what we make it, for this I have known. Love lies where we take it, no one's ever alone.

Marcel DeBie

Love is not to be purchased and affection has no price.

St. Jerome

The heart that loves is always young.

Unknown

The richest love is that which submits to the arbitration of time.

Lawrence Durrell

The symptoms of love range from having the chills to suffering from fever. Love is a fluctuating thermometer that plays tennis.

Dave Davidson

Love is the only thing you
get more of by giving it away.

Lotus

Love is the angel that wanders
within, tormenting the heart.

David Marsh

It would be impossible to "love" anyone or
anything one knew completely. Love is directed
towards what lies hidden in its object.

Paul Valéry

True love is eternal, infinite, and always like itself.
It is equal and pure, without violent demonstrations: it is
seen with white hairs and is always young in the heart.

Honore de Balzac

Love is a conflict between reflexes and reflections.

Mangnu Hirschfield

Love is a better teacher than duty.

Albert Einstein

I'm not a smart man,
but I know what love is.

Forest Gump

Love is absolute loyalty. People fade, looks fade,
but loyalty never fades. You can depend so much
on certain people, you can set your watch by them.
And that's love, even if it doesn't seem very exciting.

Sylvester Stallone

The sweetest joy the wildest woe is love.

Bailey

Love is a feeling that you're gonna have a feeling
of a feeling like you've never felt before.

Shannon Gregg

Love is everything it's cracked up to be…
It really is worth fighting for, being
brave for, risking everything for.

Erica Jong

To love and be loved is to feel
the sun from both sides.

David Viscott

The book you're reading is one of over 100 hundred books written, designed, photographed and published by Dave Davidson. From politics to poetry, coffee to comedy many titles also include his brother, Dan Davidson who is a chiropractor.

As the creative force behind the Rhymeo series the Davidson brothers share the pen name of Cyrano D. (a.k.a. Cyrano De Words-u-lac). Both brothers are energetic inspirational speakers, scripture song songwriters (PoetTree.com), radio broadcasters and social media gurus. Dave's comedy pen name is Hugh Myrrh and Dan's is Joe Kurr.

Dan and Dave's professional photography and filmmaking careers include hundreds of weddings and presidential political coverage. They have together created many brands including Rhymeo, Prezography, Think Wow, Dare Diet, Verse Rehearse, Freon Neon, Phoday, Surge Up, Inspire Me Biography, Picture Perfect You and Quotophotos.

Bestselling books in print by Dan and Dave Davidson are over one million books and include, "A Mother's Love Is Made Up Of," "Cup of Devotion With God," "Surviving Temptation Island," "If I Could Live My Life Again" and "God's Great Ambition".

Dan and Dave's life mission statement is shared double time in the acronym **T.I.M.E.** - **T**each, **I**nspire, **M**otivate and **E**ncourage & **T**rain, **I**nfluence, **M**entor and **E**quip.

For links to sharable free content, the lastest blog posts, info how to book the brothers for interviews and speaking engagements, for updates on Dave's large family of kids, publishing consulting and the most current list of over 100 published books visit

DAVEDAVIDSON.com

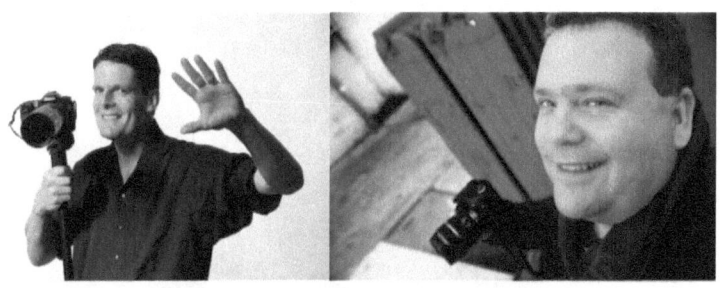

Dave@DaveDavidson.com   Dan@DanDavidson.com

Love & Romance Titles by Dave Davidson

Love Poetry Titles by Dave Davidson

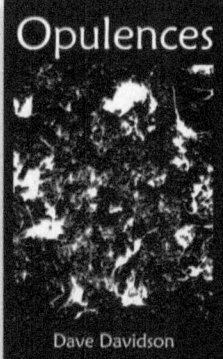

Picture Perfect Titles by Dave Davidson